NORTH YORKSHIRE BUSES

JOHN LAW

AMBERLEY

The city of York has long attracted visitors and many arrive by coach. On a nice day in 1977, up to forty or so had arrived from the Loughborough area in Oliver's Luxicoaches 618 KRA, a Yeates-bodied Bedford SB1.

First published 2019

Amberley Publishing
The Hill, Stroud
Gloucestershire, GL5 4EP

www.amberley-books.com

Copyright © John Law, 2019

The right of John Law to be identified as the Author of this work has been asserted in accordance with the Copyrights, Designs and Patents Act 1988.

ISBN 978 1 4456 8354 6 (print)
ISBN 978 1 4456 8355 3 (ebook)

All rights reserved. No part of this book may be reprinted or reproduced or utilised in any form or by any electronic, mechanical or other means, now known or hereafter invented, including photocopying and recording, or in any information storage or retrieval system, without the permission in writing from the Publishers.

British Library Cataloguing in Publication Data.
A catalogue record for this book is available from the British Library.

Origination by Amberley Publishing.
Printed in the UK.

Introduction

In land area, North Yorkshire is by far the largest of the four present-day counties that once made up the vast area of Yorkshire. Previously known as the North Riding, it lost the Middlesbrough area to Cleveland in 1974, but regained it when that was abolished in 1996. As part of the other 1974 boundary changes, North Yorkshire was formed to take over the former North Riding, the city of York and parts of the old West Riding. These included the towns of Harrogate, Skipton and Selby.

Other than stagecoaches and horse-drawn carts, public transport in the area began in 1875, using horses as motive power, but on rails owned by the Middlesbrough & Stockton Tramways Company. These were electrified in 1898 and the Yorkshire section passed to Middlesbrough Corporation in 1921, before finally ceasing in 1934.

The city of York gained its horse trams in 1880, with the small system being electrified in 1910. Trolleybus operation followed, but all had ceased by 1935 as the West Yorkshire Road Car Company (WYRCC) had taken over operations the previous year. York Corporation retained an interest in the city's public transport, forming a joint committee with WYRCC that lasted through the National Bus Company period up until the 1980s.

As well as York, WYRCC's operating area covered Harrogate, Leeds, Bradford and stretched as far east as Scarborough. Privatisation saw the West Yorkshire services pass to Yorkshire Rider and eventually become part of the First Group. Harrogate area services passed to the small AJS/Blazefield empire, later being sold to Transdev. The Yorkshire Coastliner services from Leeds and York to the seaside resorts of Whitby, Scarborough and Bridlington, along with Malton Depot, also ended up with Blazefield and Transdev. If all this seems rather complicated, the photographs within this book will help towards an explanation.

Trolleybuses were also to be found in the north of the county, running through the industrial belt along the south bank of the River Tees. These were operated by the Teesside Railless Traction Board (TRTB), which was jointly owned by Middlesbrough Corporation and Eston Urban District Council. Trolleybuses were used from 1919 until 1971, three years after TRTB was merged with Middlesbrough & Stockton Corporation Transport Departments to form Teesside Municipal Transport. This later became known as Cleveland Transit, and was to subsequently be sold to Stagecoach.

One other tramway remains to be mentioned: the Scarborough Tramway Company, a 3-foot 6-inch gauge system operated by a fleet of electric cars between 1904 and 1931, when United Automobile Services took over the routes using buses.

United Automobile Services began life in Suffolk as far back as 1912. The company also ran two routes in County Durham. Rapid expansion saw services start elsewhere in the North East and Yorkshire, as well as Lincolnshire and East Anglia. Becoming a Tilling Group operator in 1929, the East Anglian operations were renamed Eastern Counties in 1931. Being a Tilling concern, with a mainly Bristol-built fleet, control passed to the National Bus Company in 1969.

The Thatcherite policies of the 1980s saw United being split up. The company's Scarborough operations, by then named Scarborough & District, passed to East Yorkshire Motor Services (EYMS). In 1990, the services around Middlesbrough and Whitby were in the hands of Tees & District – another split from United. These eventually fell into the hands of Arriva.

Long before the days of the National Bus Company, East Yorkshire Motor Services, despite being based in Hull, had operated in North Yorkshire, reaching both Scarborough and York. This situation remains in place today, with East Yorkshire enduring as an independent concern, until the Go-Ahead Group took over in 2018.

The other former National Bus Company subsidiary to operate into what is now North Yorkshire was the West Riding Automobile Company, which had its roots in tramway operation around Wakefield. West Riding, independent until 1967, ran buses in the Selby area and northwards into York. After privatisation, Arriva eventually took over and still runs bus services there today.

The present-day situation is that all the major bus groups now operate within North Yorkshire, providing a colourful selection of vehicles. The numerous independent companies that also run stage carriage services within the county provide further variety and have done so from the early days. Many have fallen by the wayside, with Saltburn Motor Services, Percival's of Richmond, Ezra Laycock from Barnoldswick (in Lancashire, but serving Skipton) and Samuel Ledgard all now being just memories. More recent casualties include Pennine Motor Services, Leven Valley and Stephensons of Easingwold. Nevertheless, there are still plenty left to provide an adequate selection of liveries to delight most bus enthusiasts.

Finally, thanks to the late Les Flint, Keith Jenkinson, Jim Sambrooks and Peter Tuffrey for supplying a few photographs to fill in a couple of gaps in the author's collection. Thanks also to Bus Lists on the Web for providing a 'one-stop' source of information during the research for this book.

The city of York's electric tram system began operation in 1910, initially using a fleet of eighteen four-wheeled cars built by British Thompson-Houston. One of these, numbered 6, is seen when new on the Nessgate to Fulford route, which was originally operated by horses. This route, along with the rest of the system, closed in 1935. (Author's Collection)

York's small trolleybus network opened in 1915. After two generations of rather primitive electric vehicles, the system closed in 1929. However, 1931 saw the reopening of route 4 from the city centre to Heworth, using three Roe-bodied Karrier-Clough trolleybuses, illustrated here by 30 (VY 2991). When the city's trolleybuses closed permanently in January 1935, these vehicles were sold to Chesterfield Corporation for further service. (Author's Collection)

The city of York's public transport system was merged with the West Yorkshire Road Car Company in 1934, but York Corporation retained some interest and local buses in York were given the fleetname 'York West Yorkshire'. Back in the early 1960s, a Bristol K6B/ECW fifty-six-seat double-decker, fleet number YDG75 (HWW 886), built in 1949, is turning right out of Rougier Street onto Lendal Bridge. In the left background, a Hammond's Brewery dray has just unloaded outside the Lendal Bridge Inn. That establishment is still open today and is one of York's premier real ale pubs, now called The Maltings. (Les Flint)

The chassis of WYRCC's Y398 was new in 1939 as a Bristol K5G with ECW bodywork, but was rebodied, again by ECW, in 1955. It was then given fleet number YDG85 and was reregistered as OWT 198. It is seen in heavy traffic from the vantage point of the city walls, passing the end of Leeman Road, not far from Lendal Bridge and the railway station. Again photographed in the early 1960s, it is seen alongside a Bristol Lodekka, which was fairly new at the time. (Les Flint)

Bearing 'York West Yorkshire' fleetnames in the traditional style is 3794 (EWU 875C), a 1965-built Bristol Lodekka FS6B with ECW sixty-seat bodywork fitted with platform doors. It is seen at its Rougier Street stand in York city centre in 1976. Even today, Rougier Street is one of the city's main bus interchanges, others being the railway station frontage and Piccadilly, as York has never been blessed with a bus station.

When new in 1966, 'York West Yorkshire' Bristol FS6B NWU 471D was numbered YDX236. When photographed opposite York's railway station, sometime around 1977, it had received the number 3816 in National Bus Company style. Like the subject of this page's top picture, it has ECW sixty-seat bodywork.

The 'York West Yorkshire' fleet did not consist entirely of double-deck vehicles. In February 1981, under the city walls across from the railway station, we see 3235 (PYG 653E), a dual-doored Bristol RELL6G with forty-eight-seat ECW bodywork. It is about to depart for Haxby, which is in completely the opposite direction to the way it is facing!

A more modern double-deck bus to carry 'York West Yorkshire' fleetnames, 3943 (AWU 290G) was a Bristol VRT/SL6G that was bodied by ECW and seated seventy passengers. When new in 1969, it was numbered as YVR43. It was photographed in mid-1980 opposite York station.

Part of the main West Yorkshire fleet, 1165 (AWR 883G) is seen waiting outside York station in the mid-1970s, prior to a rural trip to Malton. When new in 1969, this ECW-bodied Bristol LH6L, with forty-one-seat ECW bodywork, carried fleet number LH15.

In the mid-1970s, both United and West Yorkshire used a patch of spare ground beneath the city walls of York to park their vehicles between duties. It is here that we see the latter's 1226 (NWR 721D), a fifty-four-seat Bristol RELL6G with fine-looking bodywork by ECW. Prior to the company's 1971 renumbering, it had been known as SRG26.

Another photograph from the mid-1970s is of West Yorkshire 1081 (801CWU), seen outside York station. This thirty-nine-seat Bristol MW6G/ECW coach had been new as CUG41 in 1963. It is about to load up on a city tour, which would, at one time, have been operated by a Bedford OB.

New as CRG6, this Bristol RELH6G is seen in Pickering, sometime around 1978, when it had become 505 (TWW 766F). The lines of the ECW coach bodywork look rather splendid in NBC dual-purpose livery and the coach seats should be comfortable enough for the long trip to Bradford.

Seen when almost new in late 1978, West Yorkshire 1003 (DNW 841T) is found posing outside Malton depot. This forty-four-seat Leyland National, built without the roof-mounted pod that housed the heating equipment, was a 10351B/1R, normally known as the 'B' type.

Bearing both the National Bus Company double arrow symbol and the crest of the city of York is West Yorkshire Leyland Olympian 3832 (A683 MWX), with seventy-seven-seat ECW bodywork. It was captured on film in St Leonard's Place, with the historic De Grey Rooms (originally the officers' mess of the Yorkshire Hussars) behind, in the spring of 1984.

At the same location (and on the same day) as the previous photograph is York West Yorkshire 3771 (SUB 795W), a standard Bristol VRT/SL3/6LXB with seventy-four-seat ECW bodywork. However, it is painted in a version of the old York Corporation fleet livery to celebrate fifty years of buses in the city.

By the spring of 1987, minibuses had been introduced to the West Yorkshire Road Car fleet, as illustrated by Ford Transits 117 (D526 HNW) and 131 (D538 HNW). Both had bodies fitted out by Carlyle and a seating capacity of just sixteen. They are seen outside York railway station on local 'Hoppa' routes.

With York being such a magnet for tourists, it will come as no surprise that there have long been sightseeing trips around the city. West Yorkshire's Bedford OB coaches once operated these, but by the mid-1980s open-top double-deck vehicles were the order of the day. Not many takers in Exhibition Square after a heavy summer shower in this photograph. The vehicle is West Yorkshire 1956 (FWT 956J), a 1970-built Bristol VRT/SL6G, originally with a seventy-seat ECW body, but later converted as seen. Note the 'Citibus' fleetname, which was beginning to be applied at the time.

Like many former NBC subsidiaries, West Yorkshire was later able to apply its own livery style after the mid-1980s. In March 1988, on a cold and wet day, Leyland Lynx 1202 (E325 SWY) was photographed in Harrogate bus station.

The mid-1980s saw West Yorkshire apply the name 'Northern Rose' to some of its vehicles used on coaching duties. Here, seen in York in mid-1986, is 2711 (B83 SWX), a fifty-three-seat Plaxton-bodied Leyland Tiger that was new two years earlier.

In the short-lived York City & District colour scheme we see 45 (KUB 545V), originally 2571 in the West Yorkshire fleet. New in 1980, it was a Leyland Leopard with Plaxton 'Supreme' Express coachwork. It was photographed across the road from York railway station in spring 1990. Later that year, York City & District would fall into the hands of Rider York.

Travelling back in time to around 1975, we are at Ripon's small bus station, where we see West Yorkshire 1448 (GUG 127N), a fifty-two-seat Leyland National that was almost new at the time. Ripon was, for many years, the boundary between West Yorkshire Road Car and United Automobile Services territory, and three Bristol/ECW saloons of that company are seen behind, with the magnificent cathedral forming the backdrop.

United Automobile Services had a major presence in Scarborough, where the seafront service was operated. Performing on such a duty in July 1964 is BGS4 (992 CHN). The chassis of this fine vehicle was built in 1946 as a Bristol L5G. It was lengthened in 1957 to become type LL5G and was given a new ECW thirty-nine-seat centre-entrance body. (Les Flint)

Outside of its normal operating area is United 1165 (TRN 747), photographed at Selby sometime around 1975, probably deputising for a more modern National Express coach. This Plaxton-bodied Leyland Leopard had been new as 747 with Ribble Motor Services. A West Riding Bristol VR/ECW is on service to the rear.

United 4343 (NHN 143E) sits inside the small depot at Pickering, c. 1977. This fine-looking bus is a 1967-built Bristol RELH6G with ECW bodywork that had originally contained forty-three coach seats. However, by the time of this photograph, it had been relegated to bus duties.

A second-hand vehicle in the United fleet is seen beneath York's city walls in 1977. Number 2304 (306 PFM), a Bristol MW6G bodied by ECW, had been new in 1960 as a thirty-nine-seat coach with Crosville Motor Services, numbered CMG390. Here it is in NBC red bus livery and fitted with bus seats.

An even more unusual bus to be transferred to United from another NBC fleet, 3216 (418 DCD) is seen at Scarborough in 1979. It had, of course, been new to Southdown Motor Services in 1964 as one of that company's 'Queen Mary' fully fronted Leyland PD3/4 double-deckers with bodywork by Northern Counties. Originally numbered 418, it had been delivered to Southdown as convertible to open-top configuration.

Seen during a refreshment stop in Thirsk Market Place in autumn 1980 is United 6236 (AGR 236W), which was less than three months old at the time. This Leyland Leopard has Willowbrook dual-purpose coachwork and was capable of seating forty-nine passengers. Perhaps there was time for a pint or two in the Red Bear behind, which is still open at the time of writing.

Another United vehicle in NBC dual-purpose livery, 6048 (FHN 848J) was photographed having a rest in central Middlesbrough in 1980. New in 1971, this Bristol RELH6G had a seating capacity of forty-nine in its ECW bodywork.

It is a bleak day in Scarborough in 1981 as United 631 (EHN 631J) awaits its next duty in the United bus station. Eleven years old at the time, this ECW-bodied Bristol VRT/SL6G still looks in good condition.

United followed the trend of the mid-1980s by purchasing a fleet of minibuses for local services. A typical example of this is 2411 (C411 VVN), a Mercedes L608D with twenty-seat bodywork by Reeve Burgess. It is seen on a Scarborough local service in Falsgrave Road in May 1986.

Open-top buses have long been popular in Scarborough, running from the South Bay, around the castle promontory to the North Bay, close to Peasholme Park. United 656 (YHN 656M), a Bristol VRT/SL6G with ECW bodywork, cut down to open-top in later life, was captured on film at its northern terminus. The photographer is being saluted from the upper deck. Little did that person realise that he would soon be parted with his hat!

A more unusual open-top bus in the United fleet, 4278 (PHN 178L) was found at Grosmont station in 1986. Normally confined to seafront duties, it is operating a rail replacement service for the North Yorkshire Moors Railway, as a result of a landslip in spring 1986. This Bristol RELL6G originally had fifty seats inside its ECW bodywork. It has received a version of the 1960s coach livery.

In preparation for privatisation, the National Bus Company allowed its subsidiaries to paint their buses in various new liveries. United eventually settled on a pleasant red and white colour scheme, but not before trying this rather unusual concoction of blue and red. Fortunately it did not find favour. 234 (A234 GHN), a Leyland Olympian with ECW bodywork featuring seventy dual-purpose seats, is seen at the new Middlesbrough bus station in spring 1988. By then, United had become part of the Caldaire Group.

Under Caldaire (later British Bus) ownership, United purchased this Leyland Leopard with Alexander 'Y' type bodywork. It had been new to Western SMT in Scotland as fleet number 2622 (OSJ 622R), and is seen as United 1203 in Middlesbrough bus station in spring 1989.

A rare bus in the United fleet was 1500 (B500 MPY), a Leyland-DAB Tiger Cub/ECW B46F. It was found in Saltburn town centre in spring 1988. In 1990 it was transferred into the Tees fleet and later saw service with Jim Stones in Leigh, then MacEwans in Scotland.

An unusual version of United's livery is 1454 (HDL 414N), a Bristol LHS6L with thirty-five-seat ECW bodywork. It had been new to Isle of Wight operator Southern Vectis. On a cold day in March 1988, it was found on service at Ripon's small bus station.

Passing The Buck pub in Guisborough in spring 1988 is United 6274 (E274 KEF). This Leyland Tiger/Plaxton coach had been new to the company the year before and is shown being used on the X56 service to Whitby, for which this forty-seven-seat vehicle was well suited. Sadly, The Buck was closed in 2009 and the building is now used for other purposes.

Whitby's small bus station is the location of this photograph taken in mid-1989. The subject is United 3501 (XDL799L), a Leyland National that had been new as a forty-four-seat bus with Southern Vectis.

United 1901 (GTX 761W), a short Bristol LHS6L with ECW bodywork fitted with twenty-seven dual-purpose seats, is seen in central York in summer 1992. The bus had been new as fleet number MD8026 with National Welsh, who used it on rural services in the Vale of Glamorgan. United were also employing it on similar duties, namely the 142 route to Ripon – a service today operated by Transdev.

This picture was taken in Richmond Market Place in the mid-1990s, not long before United was absorbed by Arriva. Waiting for passengers is 812 (APT 812W), an ECW-bodied Bristol VRT/SL3/6LXB. Alongside is 1532 (L532 FHN), a MAN 11.190 with Optare Vecta forty-two-seat bodywork.

In 1990, in the former county of Cleveland, the operations of United Automobile Services were split from the parent company to become Tees & District. A pleasant red and yellow livery was adopted, as illustrated by 2744 (WAO 399Y), a former Cumberland Motor Services Leyland National 2. It is seen in Middlesbrough bus station in the spring of 1991.

In mid-1997, a sea fret was enveloping Saltburn and its environs. Almost at sea level, close to the Skelton Beck and the Saltburn Miniature Railway, is Tees & District 2637 (P637 FHN). This twenty-five-seat Optare Metrorider was almost brand new at the time.

The seaside resort of Scarborough once had a small tram system, which opened in 1904, with a fleet of four-wheeled cars built by Brush. One of them, 13, is seen in rather inclement weather along the seafront, but it will soon turn inland and head for Manor Road. The system was to close in 1931, when United Automobile Services became the major operator in the town.

One more tram system remains to be mentioned in this publication, which is that of Middlesbrough Corporation. That body took over operation from the Imperial Tramways Company in 1921 and it was only a few years after that date that this postcard view of Linthorpe Road, in the town centre, was taken, with car 134 operating along the double track. Trams finished operation in 1934.

Middlesbrough Corporation Transport had a substantial motorbus fleet, part of which is illustrated in this photograph of the depot yard on 23 August 1962. Closest to the camera is 53 (ADC 653), a Leyland PD1/3 with unusual (for a municipal operator) ECW fifty-six-seat bodywork. Two Northern Counties-bodied Guy Arabs are also featured. (Les Flint)

Teesside Municipal Transport was formed in 1968 by combining the operations of Middlesbrough and Stockton Corporations and the Teesside Railless Traction Board. A visit to the Middlesbrough Corporation depot in that year revealed that most of the buses were already in the new colours of turquoise and white, having been painted before the actual date of the amalgamation. Fleet number 17 (GDC 317), a 1957-built Guy Arab IV with Northern Counties 'lowbridge' bodywork, is prominent, along with other Guy double-deckers in the depot yard.

As the name suggests, the Teesside Railless Traction Board did not run trams, but started trolleybus operation in 1919. The business was jointly owned by Middlesbrough Corporation and Eston Urban District Council, and would later be absorbed into Teesside Municipal Transport on 1 April 1968. In TMT days, but still in TRTB livery, is trolleybus 5 (GAJ 15), a Roe-bodied Sunbeam F4, which is seen passing a lovely industrial scene at South Bank on 5 March 1969. (Les Flint)

Back to 23 August 1962 and we are paying a visit to the Teesside Railless Traction Board depot at Cargo Fleet. Three Leyland motorbuses are posing for the camera. On the left is 35 (DVN 632), a Leyland-bodied PD1A, in the centre is 21 (PVN 21), a PD2/20 with Roe bodywork, while on the right we have 46 (FAJ 496), a PD2/1, again with Leyland bodywork. (Les Flint)

The Teesside Railless Traction Board trolleybus system survived under Teesside Municipal Transport until 1971, so several of the vehicles received the turquoise and white colour scheme. Illustrating that is T282 (GAJ 12), which was originally numbered 2 in the TRTB fleet. It had been new as a Sunbeam F4 in 1950, but its East Lancs body had been replaced by one built by Roe in 1963. It is seen on service in North Ormesby in March 1971. (Les Flint)

Teesside Municipal Transport soon changed its name to the more modern-sounding Cleveland Transit, adopting a new green livery. It is applied to H221 (PVN 21), a former TRTB Leyland PD2/27 with a sixty-one-seat Roe body. It was photographed at the former depot of Saltburn Motor Services (taken over in 1974) in 1975.

The takeover of Saltburn Motor Services by Cleveland Transit brought in an eclectic selection of lightweight vehicles, including 349 (ECW 110D), which is seen on service in Saltburn in 1975. This Bedford VAM5 with forty-five-seat Plaxton coachwork had been new to Tattershall of Padiham, Lancashire.

Cleveland Transit 344 (9546 PT) is found in the yard of Saltburn depot in 1976. This Bedford SB5 with Duple Super Vega forty-one-seat bodywork had come from Saltburn Motor Services, but had been new in 1962 to Venture of Consett. Alongside is 346 (ACW 549B), a Bedford SB5 Plaxton coach.

At the former TRTB depot at Cargo Fleet, *c.* 1975, is Cleveland Transit L470 (FXG 870E). This Daimler Fleetline/Northern Counties seventy-seat vehicle had been new to Middlesbrough Corporation as fleet number 70.

Cleveland Transit 372 (KXG 372L) was purchased new in 1973 as a Leyland Leopard with fifty-one-seat dual-purpose bodywork by Willowbrook. It was photographed in the Cargo Fleet depot yard in 1975. This style of Willowbrook bodywork did not find favour with many operators, including Cleveland Transit, and 372 was later rebodied, as seen on page 33.

Cleveland Transit inherited S303 (CAJ 433C) from TRTB, but by the time of this photograph, taken in March 1981, it had been transferred to Saltburn depot, where it is seen alongside sister S305 (CAJ 435C). Both were forty-five-seat Roe-bodied Leyland Leopards.

On the same March day in 1981, with horizontal sleet, Cleveland Transit S354 (TPY 925H) is seen in Saltburn depot yard. This Bedford VAM70 with forty-eight-seat Plaxton bodywork had been new to Saltburn Motor Services.

Cleveland Transit 372 (KXG 372L) was a rather odd-looking vehicle. This Leyland Leopard once carried a Willowbrook body, as illustrated on page 31. It was rebodied in 1986 by Northern Counties as a fifty-five-seat bus and is seen in its new guise at Middlesbrough bus station. After sale by Cleveland Transit, it had further service with White Ribbon in East Kilbride and then South Lancs in the St Helens area.

An unusual bus in the Cleveland Transit fleet was 317 (HPY 317N), a Ford AO609 with bodywork by Northern Counties that was not particularly pleasing to the eye. Originally fitted with twenty-five coach seats, it is seen downgraded to bus duties in central Middlesbrough in spring 1981.

Cleveland Transit did not have a vast number of minibuses during the 1980s and those that it did own tended to be used on routes to which they were suited. One such duty was a rural service in the Guisborough area, and it is in the car park of that town that 327 (E327 LHN) is found in spring 1988. This Renault S56/Northern Counties twenty-seat bus had been new earlier in the year.

Looking smart in its Cleveland Transit colours is forty-nine-seat Leyland Lynx 15 (G615 CEF), one of many in the fleet. It was photographed in Newport Road in Middlesbrough town centre in mid-1990, less than a year after delivery.

In 1994 Cleveland Transit purchased a batch of twelve Volvo B10B-58 buses with Plaxton Verde forty-eight-seat bodywork. An example, 36 (L36 HHN), is seen leaving a rain-soaked Middlesbrough bus station in September 1994.

In the later years of Cleveland Transit, the name 'Tees Valley' was used for rural routes, and it is seen here applied to 923 (HPY 423V). This Leyland Leopard/Plaxton Supreme Express fifty-three-seat coach had been new in 1980, when it was numbered 423. It is seen entering Middlesbrough bus station in September 1994. This was the month that Cleveland Transit was sold to the Stagecoach Group, and that story is told later within these pages.

West Riding Automobile Company had a depot at Selby, which made it a candidate for inclusion in this book. At that location, on 23 August 1962, is 751 (FHL 987), a rare Seddon R2 with forty-four-seat Duple Midland bodywork. It later saw service with Rowe's of Cudworth and Valley Motor Services of Bishop's Castle. (Les Flint)

At the time of the photograph at the top of this page, West Riding was still an independent company, but it sold out to the Transport Holding Company in 1967, before becoming part of the National Bus Company two years later. Seen in NBC dual-purpose livery at Selby, c. 1975, is 257 (NHL 532F), a Plaxton Derwent-bodied Leyland Leopard that was capable of seating forty-nine passengers.

The approach to Selby's railway station acted as a terminal for most of the town's bus services. It is here, in 1982, that we see 924 (VUA 474X) bearing the fleetname of 'West Riding Selby'. This Bristol VRT/SL3/6LXB with ECW H43/31F bodywork is about to depart on route 405 to Doncaster via Askern. Behind is the tower of Selby Abbey, which had survived the Dissolution of the Monasteries to become the town's parish church.

Most NBC subsidiaries celebrated the Queen's Silver Jubilee by painting some vehicles into a special livery. West Riding was no exception, though it was unusual for a single-deck bus to receive such treatment. 291 (THL 254H), a Bristol RELL6G with ECW fifty-three-seat bodywork, was photographed in Selby in, of course, 1977.

Inside Selby depot in 1977 is West Riding 612 (RWY 515F). This Northern Counties-bodied Daimler Fleetline had been new to Mexborough & Swinton in 1967.

After a period with Caldaire Holdings, West Riding was sold to British Bus in 1995. Under the latter's ownership, a batch of Volvo Olympians, bodied by Northern Counties, was received in 1996. One of these, 622 (N622 KUA), is seen in Piccadilly, York, in the summer of 1996. West Riding was soon to become part of Arriva, an organisation that is shown elsewhere within these pages.

East Yorkshire Motor Services (EYMS) have operated into York from the city of Hull for many years, serving Market Weighton and Pockington along the way. The street known as Piccadilly served as a terminal in York and that is where we see Alexander-bodied Daimler Fleetline 901 (AFT 784C), ready to depart for Hull, c. 1975. This bus had been new to Tynemouth & District, a Northern General subsidiary, in 1965.

Also at Piccadilly, York, probably on the same day, is EYMS 953 (PAT 953M), a Leyland Atlantean AN68/1R with seventy-three-seat Park Royal bodywork. The bus is seen operating route 46X, the fast service to Hull.

East Yorkshire Motor Services was privatised in 1987, by means of a management buyout. In private hands, we see coach 50 (80 EYC), named *Hull Star,* at Filey in summer 1989. Originally registered B932 MLN, this Volvo B10M-61 has Plaxton Paramount coachwork. The registration 80 EYC was later used on other vehicles.

EYMS 546 was an unusual vehicle in the fleet. New to London Country as LRC10 (B110 LPH), this ECW-bodied Leyland Olympian coach had been intended for Green Line duties. It was photographed in Filey in summer 1989, providing plenty of comfort for passengers on the long journey to Hull.

The former United depots and operations in Pickering and Scarborough were transferred to EYMS in 1987. A year later, 113 (PRA 13R) was photographed on a pleasant spring day in Pickering. Now labelled as a Scarborough & District vehicle, this Leyland Leopard with Alexander bodywork, fitted with coach seats, had been new to East Midland Motor Services.

In 1987 EYMS also took over Wallace Arnold's last stage carriage service, run by a subsidiary named Hardwicks, from Scarborough to various villages to the west. For a while the Hardwicks livery was retained, and it is seen here applied to 171 (WBN 475T), a former Lancashire United Leyland National, in central Scarborough in 1987. More Hardwicks photographs can be found on pages 82 and 83.

Another bus to bear Scarborough & District names, 793 (SGR 793V), a Bristol VRT/SL3/6LXB with seventy-four-seat ECW bodywork, is seen in Scarborough town centre in autumn 1987, having been transferred from United.

Photographed in the autumn of 1987, EYMS 39 (D39 MAG) sits in the former United bus station in Scarborough. This coach-seated Fiat/Iveco 49.10 minibus, bodied by Robin Hood, had been new in January of that year.

By mid-1995, when this photograph was taken, EYMS Scarborough local services had been rebranded using the 'Skipper' name. Leyland National Greenway rebuild 260 (IIL 2160) is seen in rather inclement conditions on Somerset Terrace. This bus had been new to EYMS as EAT 187T.

Primrose Valley Coaches, based near Filey, were also acquired by EYMS and, again, the identity was retained for a few years. In 1995, EYMS 197 (EGR 571S) wears that fleetname while it is parked up close to Scarborough railway station. This Leyland Leopard/Plaxton Supreme Express coach had been new to Northern General.

The smart modern livery of EYMS is seen to good effect on 359 (YX57 BXG), an Alexander Dennis Enviro 200 thirty-seven-seat saloon, as it heads through Westborough, the main shopping street in Scarborough, on 24 March 2010.

Here is one of the newest vehicles in the EYMS fleet, prior to the takeover by the Go-Ahead Group in June 2018. 814 (BF67 GHZ), a Volvo B5TL with MCV seventy-one-seat bodywork, is about to depart from York station on the X46 to Market Weighton and Hull on 24 May 2018.

Having taken over Cleveland Transit in the Middlesbrough area, Stagecoach is today one of the largest operators in the region. Typical of the Teesside fleet is 22026 (NK03 XJV), a MAN 18.220 with a Transbus (Alexander) forty-two-seat body. It was photographed leaving Middlesbrough's bus station on 23 April 2018.

Also found in Middlesbrough on 23 April 2018 was Stagecoach 27507 (NK05 JXF), one of the company's earlier Alexander Dennis Enviro 300 saloons. It is seen here departing on a local service.

Arriva have two areas of dominance in North Yorkshire: one is around South Teesside, where the former United/Tees & District operations were inherited, while the other is around the Selby area, which was once part of the West Riding empire. In the summer of 2000 it is in Selby, turning off Bawtry Road, that we see Arriva 151 (G140 GOL). This Duple-bodied Dennis Dart had been inherited from the fleet of Jaronda Travel, which had recently been taken over by Arriva.

At its terminal in Selby's station approach in the summer of 2001 is Arriva's 677 (X677 YUG). This seventy-nine-seat Plaxton-bodied Volvo B7TL had been new to the company in the previous year.

Up in Arriva's South Teesside territory is the large village of Great Ayton, where 1552 (M501 AJC) was photographed passing The Buck pub (close to Captain Cook's Cottage) in September 2002. This MAN 11.190/Optare saloon had been transferred from the former Crosville Wales operation.

Inside Stokesley depot in September 2002 we see Arriva 3023 (N523 XVN), a Mercedes O405 with forty-nine-seat bodywork completed by Optare. When new it had worn the red and yellow colours of Tees & District.

The forecourt of Arriva's Stokesley depot doubled as the town's bus station. In September 2002, 7280 (G757 UYT) is seen preparing to depart for Middlesbrough. This Northern Counties-bodied Leyland Olympian had been new to a London independent, Pan Atlas.

Seen in Arriva's smart Sapphire livery on 24 April 2018 is 1440 (NK10 CFA), which was photographed arriving in Redcar after a fast run from Middlesbrough on the X4 service to Whitby. Wright bodywork, recently refurbished, is fitted to a VDL SB200 chassis.

Another Arriva bus in Sapphire livery, 1560 (NK14 GEU), a forty-one-seat Wright Streetlite DF, is seen arriving at Whitby's small bus station on 26 April 2018. On the other bank of the River Esk, high on the hill, the ruins of Whitby Abbey can be seen, made famous in fiction in Bram Stoker's *Dracula*.

Arriva's latest livery is seen at Middlesbrough bus station on 23 April 2018, having been applied to 4717 (YJ10 DFP), which was part of a batch of unique Temsa Avenue forty-two-seat saloons that had been delivered to Arriva in 2009/10.

Yorkshire Rider was established to take over the bus operations of the former West Yorkshire Passenger Transport Executive. Yorkshire Rider purchased York City & District in 1990, becoming Rider York. That fleetname is applied to 8401 (M401 UUB), a Scania L113CRL with Alexander Strider forty-eight-seat bodywork. It is seen near York station in mid-1995, not long after Yorkshire Rider/Rider York had been purchased by Badgerline, and at about the same time as that organisation became known as First Group.

In autumn 1992, Yorkshire Rider 233 (G256 LWF) was photographed in Piccadilly, York. This Renault/Dodge S56 with a twenty-three-seat Reebur body had been new to Target Travel, which had been taken over in 1990.

Now displaying the First logo, Rider York 8432 (P432 YSH) is seen over the road from York station on a wet day in November 1997. This vehicle had been delivered earlier in the year and was a forty-seat Wright-bodied Scania L113CRL.

In 2006, First Bus received a dozen Volvo B7LA/Wright Streetcar articulated vehicles, each seating just forty-two people. 19008 (YK06 ATZ) is seen, not in service, by York station on 10 July 2006. These vehicles have since been withdrawn.

Park & Ride is a big thing in York, with the city centre not being designed for the motor car. First Bus run a batch of Mercedes articulated vehicles on these, plus twelve electric Optare Versa saloons. One of these, 49906 (YJ14 BHL), makes its way past the railway station on 4 May 2017.

First Bus also runs into Skipton with services from the Leeds and Bradford direction. Operating the X84 to and from Leeds is 33483 (YX66 WJG), an Alexander Dennis Enviro E40D double-decker. It is seen in central Skipton, heading for the town's bus station, on 17 May 2017.

Privatisation saw part of the former West Yorkshire Road Car Company become Harrogate & District under the ownership of the AJS/Blazefield Group. Found in Harrogate, in Station Parade in autumn 1997, is 204 (G111 VMM). This unusual bus, a Wadham Stringer-bodied Leyland Swift, had come from Luckett's of Watford.

Route 36, a frequent service from Leeds to Harrogate and Ripon, quickly became the flagship service of Harrogate & District. Dedicated to the 36 is Wright-bodied Volvo B10LE-58 372 (R372 TWR). This forty-seven-seat dual-purpose vehicle is seen in Harrogate bus station, departing for Leeds, in July 1999.

The other operation to pass into AJS/Blazefield ownership was Yorkshire Coastliner, running to Yorkshire seaside resorts from Leeds and York, with a depot at Malton. It is there, in 1995, that we see 421 (G921 WGS), a Mercedes 708D/Reebur minibus that had been transferred from another AJS/Blazefield company, County Bus & Coach.

The year 2006 saw both Harrogate & District and Yorkshire Coastliner pass into the Transdev Group. Seen with 'Transdev Harrogate & District' fleetnames, 704 (YG52 GDK) enters Skipton bus station on 22 September 2006. This Dennis Dart SLF with Alexander/Plaxton bodywork could convey twenty-nine-passengers on dual-purpose seats.

The Transdev Group has certainly brought a variety of liveries and vehicles to the roads of North Yorkshire, though this one is actually from over the border in West Yorkshire. 239 (YJ16 DWF) is a forty-seat Optare Versa saloon, from the Keighley & District fleet, and is seen in a special 'Dalesway' colour scheme in Skipton on 17 May 2017.

Transdev's Lancashire operations also run into Skipton, where we see 2779 (BF63 HCX), a Wright-bodied B9TL double-decker, now painted in a dedicated livery for the 'Witchway' route X43. On such a duty on 17 May 2017, it is about to leave Skipton bus station on a two-hour journey to Manchester via Burnley.

Even today the 36 route from Ripon to Leeds via Harrogate is one of Transdev's premier services, and new double-deck vehicles dedicated to these duties were introduced in 2016. 3617 (BL65 YYP) is seen departing from Harrogate bus station for Leeds on 4 May 2017. The latest style of Wright bodywork, seating sixty-three passengers, is fitted to a Volvo B5TL chassis.

Transdev's latest 'Harrogate Bus Company' branding is seen applied to 1837 (H16 ESU) in Harrogate on 4 May 2017. Originally registered YJ07 PDU, the vehicle was a Wright-bodied Volvo B7RLE that had been transferred from the Lancashire operations.

A recently introduced service by Transdev is the 'Cityzap', a fast operation between Leeds and York. Working this route on 2 June 2017 is 3612 (LY03 ZAP), which is seen passing the city end of Piccadilly in York. This Wright-bodied Volvo B7TL had been new with the registration YC53 MXW.

In 2016 Transdev received a batch of ten Volvo B5TL/Wright Eclipse Gemini DPH41/28F buses for the Yorkshire Coastliner services. One of them, 3632 (BT66 MVP), was photographed during a short break at Malton while operating the 840 (Leeds to Whitby) service on 23 March 2017.

Go North East vehicles can often be found in Middlesbrough bus station on the X9/X10 services towards Newcastle upon Tyne. In a dedicated livery, we see 6308 (NK67 ECD), another Volvo B5TL/Wright combination, having a rest before returning north on 23 April 2018.

A recent addition to the bus interest of Skipton is Rotala-owned Preston Bus, who run into the town from Lancashire. About to turn into the bus station on 17 May 2017 is 33002 (BT11 UWG), a Mercedes O530 saloon that had been bought from a Derbyshire operator, Dunn-Line.

Many early bus services in Britain were run by the railway companies to enable their passengers to reach places that the rails could not. The North Eastern Railway ran regular excursions out of Scarborough to Forge Valley, a local beauty spot, and that is where charabanc BT-355 is heading in this photograph taken before the outbreak of the First World War. (John Law Collection)

Many early bus operators have long since vanished. One such company was The People's Motor Service, with a route between Filey and Scarborough. Number 2 in the fleet was this saloon, seen on trade plates in an official photograph taken by the bodybuilders Barnaby of Hull. (Thanks to Peter Tuffrey for supplying this picture)

During the turbulent years after deregulation Trimdon Motor Services began running into Middlesbrough. At the town's bus station in spring 1988 is KMA 534N, a former Crosville Bristol LH6L/ECW saloon. Trimdon Motor Services was later sold to Caldaire, who owned United at the time.

Another child of deregulation was Robson Buses, which operated mainly into Stockton. However, in mid-1990 one of the company's minibuses, C210 TLY, was found in Middlesbrough. This Dodge S56/Reeve Burgess vehicle had come from car rental firm Hertz.

There were several other independents operating stage carriage services in the Teesside area during the late 1980s and early 1990s. One of them was Delta, using this ex-United Counties Bristol RELH6G/ECW saloon registered YNV 205J. It is seen in central Middlesbrough in mid-1990.

Escort was another Middlesbrough business that began running bus services. On that sunny day in mid-1990, THH 617S heads for the suburb of Marton. This Duple-bodied Leyland Leopard coach (fitted with 'grant aid' doors, making it more suitable for bus duties) had been new to Cumberland Motor Services in 1977.

Leven Valley ran several bus services in the Middlesbrough area until March 2015, when the company ceased trading. Bought new was T13 GAJ, a 2009-built Alexander Dennis Enviro twenty-nine-seat saloon. It was photographed in Middlesbrough bus station on 10 April 2010.

Leven Valley's employees were taken on by sister company Compass Royston, which is still in business at the time of writing. Operating a student service on 25 April 2018 is PBZ 8343, which has been photographed leaving Middlesbrough bus station. This VDL SB200/Wright Pulsar had been new to Claribel's of Birmingham, where it had been registered as YJ57 BOH.

Abbott's of Leeming is a long-established coaching company with around 100 vehicles in its fleet. A few of these are kept for the limited amount of stage carriage work undertaken, including the X80 route from Middlesbrough to Northallerton. Leaving Middlesbrough's bus station with the 11.00 departure on 23 April 2018 is Optare Solo SR YJ13 HHT. This thirty-three-seat vehicle had been new to the business in March 2013.

Middlesbrough operator Stagecarriage is a relative newcomer to the bus scene in the town. Seen in the bus station on 25 April 2018 while wearing a dedicated livery for the X8 service is BN12 EOX, a Mercedes O530 saloon. It had been new to Epsom Buses in Surrey.

So-called 'cherished' registrations are useful to operators in that they disguise the true age of a bus to the general public, but they sometimes make it impossible to determine the history of the vehicle. Therefore, your author has not been able to ascertain details of this Mercedes minibus, registered RIA 7809. It was photographed in the hands of Procter's of Bedale while working a service in Northallerton in summer 1997.

Procter's now trade as Dales & District and operate several services in North Yorkshire. One route is the 767, which runs from Harrogate to Leeds/Bradford Airport. Setting out on such a journey, from Harrogate bus station on 5 August 2010, is MX10 DXM, a twenty-nine-seat Alexander Dennis Enviro 200 saloon.

KJZ 13 of Dales & District was photographed in front of Northallerton's town hall on 25 April 2018. This Volvo B7RLE/Wright Pulsar saloon had come from the defunct firm Leven Valley, where it had been registered NX59 BYC.

Shaun's Minibus & Coach Hire no longer runs the Thirsk to Northallerton service, but was still doing so on 20 June 2017, when LK58 CUA was photographed in the latter location. This vehicle, an Optare Tempo saloon using hybrid technology, had previously operated for Metroline in London. (Jim Sambrooks)

A small coach operator, Dunning's of Great Ayton, once had a few interesting vehicles. Seen at the depot, c. 1975, is WJU 407. This 1960-built AEC Reliance/Willowbrook had started life as a demonstrator with the body manufacturer. Behind is a withdrawn Roe Dalesman coach, again on an AEC Reliance chassis.

Large West Yorkshire independent Samuel Ledgard once served Harrogate, and that is where JUM 373 was photographed in 1959. Much of the Ledgard fleet consisted of second-hand buses, but this Leyland PD1 was bought new in 1946. In 1967 the company sold out to West Yorkshire Road Car. (Keith Jenkinson)

Harrogate Independent Travel served the town for a few years after deregulation. Seen outside the old bus station on a local service to Knaresborough in early 1988 is E961 NMK. Purchased new in November of the previous year, this Leyland Swift had thirty-seven-seat bodywork by Wadham Stringer.

Not to be confused with the company illustrated at the top of this page, Harrogate Coach Travel nowadays has a large network of routes around North Yorkshire. Seen in its home town when heading for Ilkley on 5 August 2010 is M951 DRG. Built in 1994 for Busways (Tyneside), it was a Scania L113CRL with bodywork by Northern Counties.

Today Harrogate Coach Travel uses the name of Connexions for its stage carriage operations. On 4 May 2017, URH 806 departs from Harrogate bus station. This Scania CN94UB Omnicity had been re-registered from YN04 GMX, and had come from Nottingham City Transport.

Connexions buses can also be found in York, where Optare Solo SR YJ65 EVH is seen passing the railway station on 4 May 2017. This thirty-seat vehicle had been new to the company in 2015.

MK63 WZY, a twenty-nine-seat Alexander Dennis Enviro E20D, had been delivered to Connexions in October 2013. It was photographed passing under the city wall in York and heading for the railway station on 5 July 2017.

Durham Travel Services once operated the open-top bus service in Whitby. In September 2002, ex-Hull City Transport GAT 204N, a Roe-bodied Leyland Atlantean AN68/1R, was being employed on this service. (Jim Sambrooks)

The open-top tour of Whitby has recently been taken over by Coastal & Country Coaches, a local operator. Passing the town's small bus station on 26 April 2018 is X596 EGK. This Volvo B7TL/Plaxton had been new to London General in 2001, when its body had a roof and two doors.

Ezra Laycock was one of the pioneers of motorbus transport in the Yorkshire-Lancashire border area. Based at the small town of Barnoldswick, now in Lancashire, the operator ran a regular service into Skipton, and that is where we see WYG 540, on 19 August 1967. This Roe-bodied AEC Reliance had been new to the company in 1959. Ezra Laycock Limited was sold to Pennine Motor Services in 1972. (Les Flint)

Another bus company operating into Skipton was Silver Star, which ran a service to and from Carleton. Here is one of the company's vehicles, GOU 721, a fine Bedford OB/Duple bus. It has proved impossible to ascertain anything about this bus, originally registered in Hampshire. With it having just journeyed over the railway, Les Flint photographed it passing a superb old car to the north of Skipton, c. 1960. Silver Star sold out to Ezra Laycock in 1961.

Pennine Motor Services of Gargrave ran between Skipton, Settle and onwards into Lancaster. New to the company in 1947 was GWT 318, a Leyland Tiger PS1 with Burlingham thirty-five-seat bodywork. It was photographed in Skipton bus station in the early 1960s. (Les Flint)

MTD 235 had originally been a demonstrator with Leyland Motors, but later passed to Pennine Motor Services. This forty-one-seat Leyland Royal Tiger with centre-entrance coachwork by Leyland, which was new in 1950, is seen towards the end of its life in Settle in October 1967. (Les Flint)

After many years of operating Leyland Leopards, Pennine Motor Services turned to other types to satisfy its vehicle requirements. Purchased in 1991, H314 WUA is a Reebur-bodied Leyland Swift with thirty-nine dual-purpose seats. It is seen on a beautiful summer day on a town service at Skipton bus station in 1991. Sadly, the company ceased trading in 2014.

After the demise of Pennine Motor Services, North Yorkshire County Council began the operation of several local routes around Skipton, using their own vehicles. One of these, SF14 HBY, a Fiat minibus, is seen approaching the town's bus station on 17 May 2017.

Kirkby Lonsdale Coach Hire also now operates over roads that once saw the buses of Pennine Motor Services, running from Skipton to the company's home town. Departing from Skipton bus station and heading for Settle, again on 17 May 2017, is BN09 FWR. This Mercedes O530 has forty-two-seat bodywork and had been new to Evobus in Coventry.

Pride of the Dales was another bus company serving the town of Skipton, though the company's services had recently passed to the Transdev Group. In spring 2001, Optare Metrorider VIA 187 was photographed on service outside Skipton railway station. The registration of this bus was later transferred to an Optare Solo.

Skipton Busways was a short-lived operator that ran a town service. On such duties, at the bus station in summer 1991, is EUM 892T, a former West Riding Leyland National.

ABC Travel, a Merseyside operator, once ran a long route into Skipton bus station and that is where, in autumn 1994, we see L700 ABC. This Optare Delta-bodied DAF SB220, seating forty-nine passengers, had been new to the company earlier in that year. ABC Travel no longer exists, but other Lancashire-based bus companies still serve Skipton.

Another Lancashire independent that served North Yorkshire, Tyrer Bus, used this Volvo B7RLE with forty-three-seat Wright bodywork on its route into Skipton. That is where we see PL05 UBR on 22 September 2006, in the bus station. Tyrer Bus was sold to Holmeswood Coaches in 2013.

Lakeland Coaches, based at Clitheroe in Lancashire, once operated the X80 service to Preston from Skipton bus station, where X685 REC was photographed in spring 2001. This East Lancs-bodied DAF DE02 had been new to the company in 2000. Lakeland Coaches still exist, but no longer operates this route.

The small market town of Selby was once served by South Yorkshire Road Transport of Pontefract, but only on certain days of the week. On one of those infrequent forays in *c.* 1975, fleet number 85 (2600 WW) was photographed at Selby railway station approach, ready to head for its home town. This 'lowbridge' Leyland PD3/1 with sixty-seven-seat Roe bodywork, fitted with platform doors, was new in 1960.

Another independent to run stage carriage services into Selby is Thornes of Bubwith. These services are still operated at the time of writing, but are now fairly infrequent. Lightweight vehicles were used in the later years of the twentieth century, including a Bedford VAL bus and various other Bedford buses and coaches. HBT 378S was the registration originally applied to a Bedford YRQ/Plaxton coach, but by 1992 it had been fitted to this Bedford/Willowbrook bus, which is seen at its Selby terminus.

In the 1970s Jaronda Travel ran a service between Selby and the village of Drax. Seen departing from its Selby terminus in 1977 is SPT 358M, a Bedford YRT/Plaxton bus. It had been new to County Durham operator Gypsy Queen in 1974.

Burley's (trading as Majestic, see page 89) once ran the Selby to York via Cawood service. When that company ceased trading, Jaronda Travel took over, often using a second-hand Bristol LH. Dennis Darts were later employed, and one of these, P212 RWR, a forty-seat Plaxton-bodied example bought new in 1997, is seen in Piccadilly, York, in the spring of 1998. Jaronda Travel was later sold to Arriva.

An operator trading as Steve Stockdale ran a few stage carriage services in the Selby and Goole areas in the 1980s. Seen at the former location in summer 1988 is RNY 103M, a former Cardiff City Transport Seddon Pennine 4 midibus with dual-purpose bodywork capable of seating twenty-five passengers.

Stanley Moore once operated a bus route between Selby and Cawood, via Wistow, following the route of a long-closed light railway. Seen on service in Selby in February 1981 is VWX 696L, a Bedford YRQ/Plaxton Elite forty-five-seat coach that was bought new by the operator in 1973.

Primrose Valley Coaches once ran a service into Filey from the area near Hunmanby. A variety of buses was owned, but a rare one to illustrate the fleet is NAH 661F, seen at the depot in 1979. This Bedford VAM5 with ECW bodywork had been new to Eastern Counties in Norfolk. The Primrose Valley service was later taken over by East Yorkshire Motor Services but the fleetname was retained for a short while.

Lovitt's of Filey is, today, a renowned fish merchant in the seaside town. Whether this bus operator is any relation is not known, but in the summer of 1989 it was running a town circular service using a tiny Bedford minicoach. The example on the left, RTO 820G, was probably the spare vehicle for the day. This Bedford J2/Plaxton coach had been new to Skill's of Nottingham. On its right is MFR 497F, a former Abbott's of Blackpool AEC Reliance/Plaxton coach.

In the 1990s, in competition with East Yorkshire and Shoreline Suncruisers, Appleby's ran the open-top seafront service connecting both bays in Scarborough. Though its headquarters was in Lincolnshire, the firm also had an operating base in Yorkshire. Seen at the South Bay terminus in August 1992 is WFM 159K. This Daimler Fleetline/Northern Counties coach had been new to Chester City Transport.

Appleby's also ran normal stage carriage services in the Scarborough area. In late 1996, in the town centre, we see MGR 915T, a fifty-five-seat Leyland Leopard/Duple Dominant bus that was new to Trimdon Motor Services, County Durham. Appleby's have since ceased trading.

Shoreline Suncruisers operates the seafront service in Scarborough using a fleet of open-top buses. Even today, the route operates in competition with East Yorkshire. At the southern terminus in summer 1992 is HPK 507N, a former Alder Valley Bristol VRT/SL2 with ECW bodywork.

At the stop nearest to Scarborough town centre on 24 March 2010 is Shoreline Suncruisers B227 WUL. This MCW Metrobus was once in the London Buses fleet as M1227.

Wallace Arnold was mainly a coach operator. Based in Leeds, it was famous for its well-organised holiday tours, both in the UK and abroad. It also ran stage carriage services in Yorkshire, using the fleetnames of firms it had taken over. The last of these was Hardwicks, running into Scarborough, where, in summer 1979, KUM 512L is seen between duties. Wearing both WA and Hardwicks fleetnames, this fifty-three-seat Leyland Leopard/Plaxton Elite Express had been delivered in 1973.

In mid-1986, a Hardwicks coach is about to depart from Falsgrave Road in Scarborough for Ebberston. PNW 312W is a Leyland Leopard/Plaxton Supreme Express coach, which was new to Wallace Arnold, but now showing no sign of that ownership. In 1987 the Hardwicks operation was sold to East Yorkshire Motor Services.

Wallace Arnold coaches were, of course, frequent visitors to North Yorkshire. A very unusual vehicle to take tourists to the North Yorkshire Moors Railway was DLC 950J, a Mercedes O302 forty-seven-seat coach, which was photographed outside the Station Hotel in Grosmont in 1976.

Because Guide Friday had begun operating city tours in Edinburgh, Lothian Regional Transport, the Scottish capital's principal bus operator, retaliated by running competitive tours of various cities in the UK, including York. One of the many open-top Leyland Atlanteans in the fleet, 925 (OSF 925M) is seen in autumn 1992 with Monkgate Bar behind. It is being operated in conjunction with Jorvik Viking Tours (see page 85).

Like Lothian Regional Transport, Guide Friday used vehicles of another operator (in this case Top-Line) in their livery for city tours of York. LBO 501X is in a pleasant version of the Guide Friday livery as it passes the De Grey Rooms on St Leonards Place on 11 July 2006. This Leyland Olympian with East Lancs bodywork had been new to Cardiff City Transport as fleet number 501 in 1981. It was converted to open-top much later.

One of the many operators that have served the tourists in York is Jorvik Viking Tours, which used open-top double-deckers. Typical of those running in mid-1991 is GDR 210N, a former Plymouth City Transport Leyland Atlantean AN68/1R, originally with a covered body built by Park Royal. It is seen passing the railway station.

An earlier Atlantean with Jorvik, again from Plymouth, WJY 758 had been new as a PDR1/1 with sixty-seven-seat bodywork by Metro-Cammell. In open-top condition, it is seen at Exhibition Square in autumn 1997.

A short-lived operator to attempt stage carriage services in York was Acomb Link. In the spring of 1990, it was using GHB 176J, a former Merthyr Tydfil Transport Leyland Leopard with East Lancs bodywork. The coach is seen about to depart from opposite York railway station.

It has proved impossible to ascertain details of Ryedale Link, who ran a Strensall to York 'taxibus' service using this tiny Isuzu/Bedford minibus. Registered F201 XUM, it was photographed in the city centre in 1989 during the few months it was in operation.

For several years after deregulation, Glenn Line ran a number of competitive services, using York station forecourt as a terminus. At first various Leyland Leopard coaches were employed, but in summer 1997 a more suitable vehicle was being employed. Seen as it sets out for the suburbs, DPH 499T, a forty-one-seat Leyland National, had been new to London Country as SNB 499 in 1979.

Back in the 1970s, Gorwood Brothers ran an infrequent stage carriage service into York using various Bedford coaches. In 1977, VCT 547, a 1962-built Bedford SB5/Duple Super Vega, is seen parked up in Layerthorpe, York. It had been new to Lincolnshire operator Gem Coaches (Blankley) of Colsterworth.

Reliance, based at Stockton-on-the Forest, has long operated a service towards Helmsley from York – a situation still in place today. Back in 1974, or thereabouts, APY 386K is seen parked in the company's depot yard. Unusually for an independent, this Seddon Pennine RU with fifty-one-seat Seddon bodywork had been bought new in 1972.

Reliance's fleet later consisted of lightweight Bedfords, but by autumn 1997, when R26 GNW was photographed at Exhibition Square in York, these had been replaced. Purchased new in that year, R26 GNW was a DAF SB220 with Optare fifty-two-seat bodywork. More recent vehicles for the bus services include several Wright-bodied saloons.

Majestic (Burley) of Cawood once ran a regular bus service between Selby and York via its home village. For many years, lightweight buses were used on this route. Back in 1974, CWT 451B is seen in Micklegate, Selby, the company's terminus – most other buses used the railway station approach. This bus, which had been bought new in 1964, was a Bedford SB5 with a Willowbrook forty-two-seat body.

In York city centre, Majestic shared Merchantgate with York Pullman and other operators as a terminal point. It is here, c. 1977, that we see OWX 396K, a Willowbrook-bodied Bedford YRQ forty-five-seater. This route was later to pass to Jaronda Travel, and it is now in the hands of Arriva.

French-owned Veolia was not really an independent, but is included here for completeness. For a few years the company operated a few services in the York area and, on 1 May 2007, L779 SNO is seen in the city centre. This Leyland Olympian/Alexander 'R' type bus had been new to Dublin bus as fleet number RH171, registered 93-D-10172. Veolia later sold their operations to Transdev.

Vyner House Coaches was a York-based operator. A most unusual vehicle in the fleet was TDN 110N, a Seddon Pennine IV with Seddon bodywork that was fitted with twenty-five coach seats. New in 1974, it is seen in a central York coach park just before nightfall, c. 1975.

Another sightseeing operator in York was Viking Tours, operating a mainly Bristol-built fleet of open-top buses. One such vehicle, DRX 122C, a former Thames Valley Bristol FLF6G/ECW, is seen squeezing between the tourists on Stonebow, in central York, in August 1993.

Stephensons of Easingwold once ran several stage carriage services into the city of York. Seen here beside Exhibition Square on 1 May 2007 is S159 JUA. This DAF SB220 with Optare 'Delta' bodywork had been new to Speedlink Air Services, from the London area, despite the Yorkshire registration. In early 2018, Stephensons ceased operating and the services passed to York Pullman (see page 95).

York Pullman was a bus company founded in the 1920s and eventually developed a small network of routes radiating from York. The vehicles were based at a purpose-built depot in Navigation Road, but in 1951 a small office was established in Bootham Tower, under the city walls, beside Exhibition Square. Many of the company's bus services terminated and started from here. On 19 May 1968, AEC Regent III/Roe 64 (JDN 668) is posed outside the depot. This fine double-decker was later preserved by the late Tony Peart and still survives in fine fettle today. (Les Flint)

Some of York Pullman's services used Merchantgate as the York terminus, and it is here, in 1977, that we see 87 (TDN 387H) awaiting departure for Stamford Bridge. New to the company in 1969, this AEC Swift had fifty-two-seat bodywork that was partly built by Park Royal, but completed in Yorkshire by C. H. Roe.

In its later years, York Pullman turned to lightweight vehicles, an example of which is 110 (SVY 252N), a Bedford YRT with fifty-five-seat Plaxton 'Derwent' bodywork. It is seen reversing onto its stand at York's Exhibition Square in 1980.

In 1985, York Pullman was sold to Reynard's Coaches, which was then renamed Reynard-Pullman. That fleetname is seen applied to E575 ANE, photographed departing from Harrogate bus station in August 1989. Originally a demonstrator, this vehicle was a Renault S56 with twenty-eight semi-coach seats in a Northern Counties body.

In this photograph, taken at York station *c.* 1990, just the Reynard name is applied to CSU 244. This Leyland Leopard, originally registered REL 402R, had been new to National Travel (South West) and was fitted with a Willowbrook 'Spacecar' body. It was later rebodied by Plaxton as a fifty-five-seat bus and entered the fleet of York Brothers of Cogenhoe, Northamptonshire, prior to being sold to Reynard. When Reynard was sold to Yorkshire Rider in 1990, CSU 244 was transferred to Brewers, a South Wales operator.

Reynard sold the York Pullman name and several coaches to Kingston-upon-Hull City Transport (KHCT) in early 1990. Bearing the famous fleet identity is KHCT 201 (H201 XKH), a Reebur-bodied thirty-seven-seat Leyland Swift. Named *Joseph Hansom* after the York-born inventor of the hansom cab, it is seen picking up a group of tourists at York station in autumn 1992.

In preparation for privatisation, KHCT sold its York Pullman operations to Durham Travel Services in 1993, who took on some council-tendered city services. With the fleetname of 'Pullman Easylink', Dennis Dart SLF/Plaxton thirty-three-seat saloon R132 FUP is seen loading up opposite York station in spring 1998. Sister bus R120 FUP is about to overtake. These operations passed to First York in 2000.

The latest business calling itself York Pullman was that of Tom James of K&J Travel of York, but this has now been renamed as The York Pullman Bus Company Ltd. Having been in business for over ten years, there has been considerable expansion, including the purchase of the services of Stephensons of Easingwold in 2018. Tapping into the lucrative tourist trade in York, 214 (BYX 143V) was seen opposite the railway station on 29 June 2008. This MCW Metrobus had been new to London Transport as M143 in 1979, long before it was converted to open-top.

Looking resplendent in traditional colours, 254 (W666 WMS) is seen passing the original York Pullman offices in Exhibition Square, York, on 11 May 2009. New in 2000, this DAF SB220 with Ikarus bodywork had come from County Durham independent Weardale Motor Services, hence the rather unusual registration. Most of York Pullman's bus routes were sold to Transdev in early 2012.

In the last couple of years, York Pullman has returned to stage carriage work, operating various routes, including the 36 to Pocklington/Sutton upon Derwent. On 5 July 2017, the new-bought vehicle for this route is seen just after setting out from York railway station. A Volvo B8RLE with forty-six-seat MCV bodywork, it was registered BV17 CPU and painted into a dedicated livery for the service.